ONCE UPON A DREAM

Library of Congress Catalog Card Number: 98-90242

ISBN: 0-9708726-0-7

First edition

Summary: Children's poetry, fantasy

CONTENTS

UPON A DREAM

Would you like to take a journey with me ?
Let's open the door,
You have the key.
Close your eyes, and take my hand.
Off we'll go
To another land.
Some place special,
Where dreamers go.
Some place special,
That others don't know.
In a field,
Or beside a stream.
Anywhere upon a dream.

THE SPECIAL PLACE

There is a special place
Only YOU can go.
How do you get there?
Only YOU know.
A special place
That has yet to be explored
And when you're there
You will never get bored.
You can go in the day,
Or at night in your bed,
You can go anytime
Just use your head.
Fantastic wonders
And magic you'll find
Waiting for you
inside of your mind.

MY FAVORITE TREE

Down the hill,
Across the stream,
A little farther
And I can dream.
No one else,
No one but me
Sits beside my favorite tree.
She's tall, strong,
And very old,
Wonderfully wise and bold.
Oh how good
It feels to be
Here beside my favorite tree.
I lean back and close my eyes,
She whispers softly
And tells no lies.
Talking back
Into the wood
Always I am understood.
Everything is alive and free
Here beside my favorite tree.
There is no place
I'd rather be,
Than here beside my favorite tree.

WHAT IF?

What if everybody had a star?
It could be close,
It could be far.
It wouldn't matter who you are,
Everyone would have a star.
And when you'd look
In the sky at night,
You would see your star shining bright.
A new star seen
In the early morn',
Meant somewhere close
A child was born.
Who's to say?
It could be true.
That in the sky,
A star shines for you.

ON MY BIKE

I had a bad day,
But I'm on my bike
The clouds that were gray
Have all blown away,
Now it's time to play
And I'm on my bike.
Flying through the air,
And I'm on my bike.
Wind in my hair,
A feeling I must share,
Lots of time to spare
When I'm on my bike.
Floating out in space
And I'm on my bike.
A smile on my face,
A star I could chase,
I can go anyplace
When I'm on my bike.

A FRIEND

A friend is there,
When no one is around,
To give you a smile,
When none can be found.
A friend you can tell
A secret to,
And always know
She'll keep it true.
A friend is one
Who cares how you feel.
And hopes that all
Your wounds will heal.
You can share an idea,
Big or small
Or with a friend you can sit
And say nothing at all.
A friend is sad
When you move away.
And for that friend,
You wish you could stay.
Always have
A hand to lend.
And save some time
For a friend.

IN A BOOK

If you've got some time to spare
Grab a book and find a chair,
For in the pages of a book
You can sail with Captain Hook,
Sit atop a horse that flies
Or in a sub with foreign spies
See the world long ago,
Travel through the ice and snow.
You could go to the moon
And take a walk,
Or climb up on the great beanstalk.
You my friend
Can plant Jack's seed,
Just grab a book
And begin to read.

HUG SOMEONE

Hug someone you love
For no reason at all,
Hug someone who's hurting
After a fall.
Hug someone
With a tear in their eye,
Hug someone
To say goodbye.
Then on a day
When you're feeling blue,
SOMEONE comes along
With a hug for you.

I LIKE TO PRETEND

I like to pretend
That I can fly,
Just like a bird
Across the sky
I like to pretend,
Would you like to try?
You could pretend
You're horse by the sea
Running, running, running so free,
And when you pretend,
That horse you can be.
I like to pretend
I'm a fish in a stream,
I like to pretend
I like to dream.

Wanna trade?

A handful of marbles
To trade with you
I'll give you a green
Or two reds
For a blue.
And trading cards,
I have a lot
Would you like to see
The ones that I've got?
Or some shiny rocks
That I found by the sea.
Have you got any stones
To trade with me?
Even if you have
Nothing to bring,
Come on over
Without a thing,
'Cause best of all
What can't be bought,
We could sit down
And trade a thought.

SHARING

Sharing is giving
Some of what you've got
To someone else
Who has not.
You can share a bite,
A sip,
Or a snack.
You can share with someone
Who can't share back.
On your new sled,
You could share a ride.
Why?
Because sharing feels good inside.
And feelings, you can always share.
Like telling a friend
That you care.
As the day goes on,
Remember all the while,
You can share yourself
With a smile.

PUPPY LOVE

Puppy love is honest and true,
As the world is round
And the sky is blue,
He cries when you leave,
Tugs on your sleeve,
And is always happy,
To see you.
Puppy love is gentle and kind
And not at all hard to find,
Every day
Its time to play,
And you never really
Seem to mind.
Puppy love
Is always there
So much,
Enough to share,
So with a puppy
Take good care.

MY ROOM

It's raining out,
The sun is away,
And nobody wants
To play today.
My room is a castle
Or a fortress of gold,
With a thousand stories
Yet to be told.
With a king,
A queen,
Or a knight for a friend
And all day with ME,
They would love to spend.
A rainy day
Can be lots of fun,
For in my room
There shines a sun.

Four Seasons

The stars shine bright
On a cold winter's night
And the snowy owl, he takes to flight.
Morning in spring
Is a wonderful thing
And the birds they all come out to sing.
A summer afternoon
In the month of June,
And the wind it whispers a lazy tune.
The trees so tall
With the colors of fall,
If you listen you may hear an angel call......
And a year has gone by.

SUMMER VACATION

Summer vacation is finally here,
And what a wonderful time of year.
A hot afternoon,
But the lake is cool.
And everybody is home from school.
I could go climb my favorite tree.
And look out as far as the eye can see.
On my bike,
I could go for a ride.
To the park?
To the beach?
I can't decide.
I could go play a game of ball,
Or I could sit and do nothing at all.
And its O.K.
If the sky is gray.
In my room,
I could play all day.
Maybe I'll go trade some things
With a friend.
For it is summer,
And I have some time to spend.

Shilo Publishing

5505 Valmont, Suite #35
Boulder, Colorado 80301
www.readshilo.com

Mail order

Customer

Name _____

Address _____

City _____ State _____ ZIP _____

Phone _____

Date _____

Use any orderform or visit our website for more product information.

www.readshilo.com

QUALITY CHILDREN'S BOOKS,
BOOKMARKS, CALANDERS,
CLASSROOM POSTERS,
LESSON PLANS

www.readshilo.com
Resources for teachers,
counselors, and
homeschool educators.

Your source for unique,
thought provoking
literary works.

Qty	Description			Price	TOTAL
	ONCE UPON A DREAM	softcover	ISBN: 0-9708726-0-7	$15.95	
	ONCE UPON A DREAM	hardbound	ISBN: 0-9708726-1-5	$21.95	
	TWICE UPON A DREAM	softcover	ISBN: 0-9708726-2-3	$15.95	
	TWICE UPON A DREAM	hardbound	ISBN: 0-9708726-3-1	$21.95	
			SubTotal		
			shipping included		
			Colorado Residents Add 4.15% Tax		
			TOTAL		

SHIP TO: _____
_____
_____
_____
_____

Please Send Check or Money Order
Allow 3-4 weeks for delivery

" It starts with a dream "

Raine

Raine Catalano lives with her family in beautiful Boulder, Colorado. She grew up in New England, where she first visited all the wonderful places explored in <u>Once Upon A Dream.</u>

Some of them, like her favorite tree, really exist just down the hill and across the stream. While some of the others were inspired by everyday things, that with a little imagination, aren't always what they seem.

So this book is written with the child in mind: from the youngest child, just beginning to dream, to the eighty-year-old child who still likes to pretend.

www.ingramcontent.com/pod-product-compliance
Lightning Source LLC
Chambersburg PA
CBHW041549040426
42447CB00002B/114